Countries of the World

Egypt

by Kathleen W. Deady

Bridgestone Books
an imprint of Capstone Press
Mankato, Minnesota

Bridgestone Books are published by Capstone Press
151 Good Counsel Drive, P.O. Box 669, Mankato, Minnesota 56002
http://www.capstone-press.com

Library of Congress Cataloging-in-Publication Data
Deady, Kathleen W.
    Egypt/by Kathleen W. Deady.
    p. cm.—(Countries of the world)
    Includes bibliographical references and index.
    Summary: Introduces the geography, history, animals, food, and culture of Egypt.
    ISBN 0-7368-0626-1
    1. Egypt—Juvenile literature. [1. Egypt.] I. Title. II. Countries of the world (Mankato, Minn.)
DT49 .D33 2001
962—dc21   00-024429

Editorial Credits
Tom Adamson, editor; Timothy Halldin, designer; Sara Sinnard and Timothy Halldin,
    illustrators; Heidi Schoof and Kimberly Danger, photo researchers

Photo Credits
Index Stock Imagery, 5 (bottom)
International Stock/Tom & Michelle Grimm, 16
John Elk III, 8, 14, 20
Robert Maust/Photo Agora, 6
Sean Sprague/Photo Agora, 12
StockHaus Limited, 5 (top)
Trip/A. Tovy, cover; T. Bognar, 10
Visuals Unlimited/Elliot Kornberg, 18

**Bridgestone Books thanks Jere L. Bacharach, Director of the Jackson School of International
Studies at the University of Washington, for his assistance with this project.**

1 2 3 4 5 6 06 05 04 03 02 01

Table of Contents

Fast Facts. 4
Maps 4
Flag 5
Currency 5

The Land 7
Ancient Egypt 9
Life at Home 11
Going to School 13
Egyptian Food 15
Clothing 17
Animals 19
Holidays and Celebrations 21

Hands On: Play the Snake Game 22
Learn to Speak Arabic 23
Words to Know 23
Read More 24
Useful Addresses and Internet Sites 24
Index 24

Fast Facts

Name: Arab Republic of Egypt

Capital: Cairo

Population: More than 67 million

Language: Arabic

Religion: Mostly Islam, some Christian

Size: 386,660 square miles
(1,001,450 square kilometers)

Egypt is larger than the U.S. states of Texas and New Mexico combined.

Crops: Cotton, rice, corn, wheat

Maps

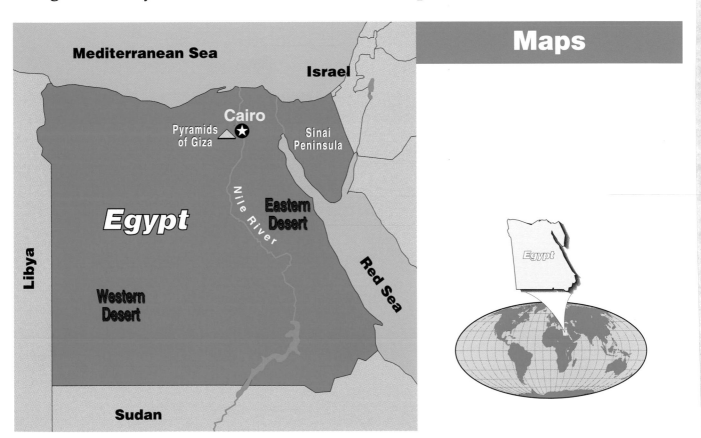

Flag

The Egyptian flag has three stripes. The stripes are red, white, and black. Red stands for struggle and sacrifice. White means purity. Black represents history. A golden eagle and shield are in the center of the white stripe. This symbol is called the eagle of Saladin. Saladin ruled Egypt in the 1100s. Egypt's government adopted the flag on October 4, 1984.

Currency

Egypt's unit of currency is the Egyptian pound. One hundred piasters equal one pound.

In 2000, about 3.4 Egyptian pounds equaled 1 U.S. dollar. About 2.3 Egyptian pounds equaled 1 Canadian dollar.

5

The Land

Egypt is a country in northeastern Africa that borders the Mediterranean Sea. Sudan is south of Egypt. Libya lies to the west. The Red Sea and Israel border Egypt on the east.

Egypt has four land regions. The Western Desert and Eastern Desert cover most of Egypt. Strong winds blow the desert sand into large piles called sand dunes.

The Sinai Peninsula is a region in northeastern Egypt. Rugged mountains rise more than 8,600 feet (2,620 meters) above sea level in the southern part of this region.

Egypt's fourth land region is the Nile Valley and Delta. The Nile is the world's longest river. The Nile River flows north through Egypt. The river then splits into many branches north of Cairo to form the Delta. About 99 percent of Egyptians live along the Nile.

The Nile Valley is the most important region in Egypt.

Ancient Egypt

The first settlements in Egypt developed along the Nile River about 5,000 years ago. Ancient Egyptians found good uses for their resources. They built irrigation systems along the Nile River to help them grow crops. These canals carried water to farms near the river.

Egyptians invented the first writing system. This system used pictures called hieroglyphics. Each picture had a certain meaning. Egyptians also created the first paper. They harvested papyrus plants that grew near the Nile and made them into paper.

Ancient Egyptians built pyramids. These huge structures held the tombs of Egyptian rulers called pharaohs. Workers built the pyramids with stone blocks. Many blocks weighed more than 2.5 tons (2.3 metric tons). The largest pyramid is in Giza. The structure is about 450 feet (137 meters) tall and took 20 years to build.

The pyramids of Giza are at least 4,500 years old.

Life at Home

Many Egyptians live in country villages. Most of these citizens are farmers called fellahin (fel-la-HEEN). Fellahin once made their houses of straw. They now use sun-baked mud bricks. Their homes may not have electricity or running water. They once farmed with simple tools and animals. They now use tractors and other modern equipment.

Fellahin families often are large. The children take care of the animals and do other chores. Many family members live together or in the same village.

Most other Egyptians live and work in crowded cities. Most of the people live in apartment buildings. Some apartments are large. Others are very small and crowded.

Cairo is the largest city in Egypt and in Africa. Cairo is noisy. The air is dirty. Cars, trucks, and even a few donkey carts crowd the streets.

Fellahin live in small villages near the Nile River.

Going to School

Egyptian children must attend primary school from age 6 to 12. In primary school, children learn reading, writing, and math for two years. They study science and the Quran (kur-AHN) in the third year. The Quran is the holy book of the Islam religion. Students also learn a foreign language, usually English.

Students in villages also learn other skills. Girls learn cooking, sewing, and embroidery. Boys learn how to farm and how to work with metal and leather.

Only about half of all students continue their education past primary school. They may attend either a general school or a specialized school. General schools prepare students for a university. Specialized schools prepare them for a trade or technical school.

Children go to primary school from age 6 to 12.

Egyptian Food

Egyptian food is simple and hearty. Most meals include a dish made with fava (FAH-vah) beans. Fava beans are boiled for hours to soften them. They are mixed with herbs and spices to make foul (FOOL), the national dish. Fava beans also are used in ta'miya (ta-MEE-ya). Ta'miya is fried balls of chickpeas, wheat, and fava beans.

Egyptians also include meat in some meals. They eat chicken or lamb with vegetables. Seafood also is popular. Beef is expensive and rare. Egyptians consider beef to be food that only wealthy people eat. Muslims do not eat pork or ham because their religion does not allow it.

Egyptian flat bread is served with every meal. The Arabic word for bread is aish (AYSH). Aish also is the word for life.

Some Egyptians sell aish in outdoor marketplaces.

Clothing

Egyptians wear many styles of clothing. In villages, people wear more traditional clothing. Modern clothing is common in cities.

Traditional clothing for men is the galabea (gahl-uh-BAY-yuh). This long loose shirt reaches to the ankles. The galabea may be white, beige, gray, or light blue. The galabea often covers cotton pants. Some men wear a skullcap. The skullcap is a sign of their Muslim beliefs.

Women may wear the traditional hijab (hee-JAHB). This scarf covers a woman's head. Only her face remains uncovered. Women wear the hijab to show their Muslim faith.

Many Egyptians wear the same kinds of clothes North Americans wear. Businessmen wear suits and ties. Businesswomen wear dresses or suits. Some wealthy people wear the latest European fashions. Children often mix modern and traditional styles.

Many Egyptian men wear a galabea.

Animals

Camels once were the most common animals in Egypt. They carried goods across deserts and on busy city streets. Camels can drink 25 gallons (95 liters) of water at one time. Their bodies store this water. Camels may travel for days without drinking again.

Farmers raise goats and sheep for milk, meat, and wool. Farmers also raise chickens, pigeons, and ducks for food.

Egypt has many wild animals. Snakes and lizards hide under rocks. Other animals live in the wetlands along the Nile. Herons, storks, and cranes feed on the river's fish. Falcons, eagles, and vultures hunt overhead for prey.

Some wild animals are nearly extinct. Crocodiles once lived along the Nile riverbanks. Gazelles, jackals, and foxes roamed the desert. A few mountain goats called ibex climb the rocky slopes of the Sinai Peninsula.

Ibex are wild mountain goats that live in the Sinai.

Holidays and Celebrations

Most Egyptians are Muslims. Muslims celebrate the month of Ramadan. They honor the time when Allah (ah-LAH) spoke to the prophet Muhammad. Allah is the Arabic word for God.

During Ramadan, Muslims fast during daylight. Each day at sundown they have a feast called iftar (IF-tar). Throughout this month, Muslims give meat to the poor. The celebration ends with a three-day holiday called Eid el-Fitr (EYE-eed el-FIT-er). Muslims make special meals and give gifts to family and friends on this holiday.

Moulid el-Nabi (MOO-led el-NAH-bee) celebrates Muhammad's birthday. Cities hold street festivals. Families decorate their homes and eat special meals.

Egyptians celebrate the Anniversary of the Revolution on July 23. The monarchy ended in Egypt on this date in 1952. Instead of a king, a president now leads the country.

Muslims follow the religion of Islam.

Hands On: Play the Snake Game

The snake game was a favorite game in ancient Egypt. The rules are simple. You can make a modern version of this game.

What You Need

Tag board
Pencil
Scissors
Markers

Game pieces
1 die
2 to 4 players

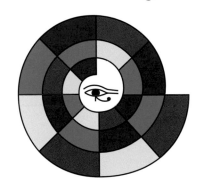

What You Do

1. Draw a large circle on the tag board. Cut out the tag board circle. Draw an eye in the middle. Draw a line like a coiled snake in a spiral from the eye to the outside edge.
2. Draw lines to divide the snake into sections. These sections will be the spaces on the game board. Color the snake. Make each section or space a different color.
3. Place the game pieces on the eye. Players take turns rolling the die. Move that number of spaces around the board. If you land on another player's space, you lose your next turn. The first player to get to the outside of the game board wins.
4. Be creative. Add spaces such as Lose a Turn or Go Back Two Spaces. Make up your own new game.

Learn to Speak Arabic

good-bye	ma salaama	(MAH sah-LAH-mah)
hello	assalaamu aleikum	(ah-sah-LA-moo ah-LAY-koom)
marketplace	souq	(SOOK)
no	la	(LA)
thank you	shukran	(shoo-KRAHN)
yes	aywa	(EYE-wah)

Words to Know

delta (DEL-tuh)—the area where a river meets the sea; the Nile River splits into many smaller branches to form a delta.

extinct (ek-STINGKT)—no longer living anywhere in the world

fast (FAST)—to give up eating for a certain amount of time

monarchy (MON-ar-kee)—a government led by a king or a queen

peninsula (puh-NIN-suh-luh)—land surrounded by water on three sides

pharaoh (FAIR-oh)—the title of the kings of ancient Egypt

prophet (PROF-it)—a person who speaks or claims to speak for God

sea level (SEE LEV-uhl)—the average level of the ocean's surface

tomb (TOOM)—a grave, room, or building that holds a dead body

Read More

Berg, Elizabeth. *Egypt.* Festivals of the World. Milwaukee: Gareth Stevens, 1997.

Heinrichs, Ann. *Egypt.* Enchantment of the World. New York: Children's Press, 1997.

Useful Addresses and Internet Sites

Egyptian Embassy
454 Laurier Avenue East
Ottawa, ON K1N 6R3
Canada

**Embassy of the Arab
    Republic of Egypt**
3521 International Court NW
Washington, DC 20008

The Ancient Egyptian Culture Exhibit
http://emuseum.mankato.msus.edu/prehistory/egypt/index.shtml
Egypt State Information Service
http://www.us.sis.gov.eg

Index

aish, 15
Allah, 21
Cairo, 11
fava beans, 15
fellahin, 11
foul, 15
galabea, 17
hieroglyphics, 9

hijab, 17
Muhammad, 21
Muslims, 15, 21
Nile River, 7, 9, 19
papyrus, 9
pyramid, 9
Quran, 13
Sinai Peninsula, 7, 19